GIFTS NURTURE LOVE

تهادوا تحابّوا

زياب ودانة مع كهرمان

DIAB AND DANA WITH KAHRAMAN

سلسلة أصدقاء الطبيعة

FRIENDS OF NATURE SERIES

AF444302

E-ISBN: 978-9948-19-418-7
Print-ISBN: 978-9948-15-195-1

GIFTS NURTURE LOVE   تَهَادَوْا تَحَابُّوا
زياب ودانة مع كهرمان
DIAB AND DANA WITH KAHRAMAN
To My Parents and My Wife

هذا صباحُ يومٍ جديد..
ذيابٌ يضيءُ مصباحَ الغرفةِ وينادي:
هيا استيقظي يا دانة!
الماما تُحضّرُ لنا الفطور،
ولا نريد أن نتأخر على المدرسة...

It is a new day...
Diab turns on the light in the room
"Wake up Dana!
Mum is preparing breakfast
and we shouldn't be late for school," he said.

أنا ذياب، وهذه أختي دانة
ونحنُ نُحبُ بعضَنا كثيراً.
وكهرمانُ صديقُنا يستيقظُ معنا،
ويأتي كلَّ يومٍ لزيارتنا
فهو يضيءُ لنا الأنوار.

My name is Diab
and this is my sister Dana.
We love each other so much.
Our friend, Kahraman, wakes up with us
He visits us every day
because he turns lights on for us.

تقول دانة :
ـ لقد تأخَّرَ كهرمانُ اليومَ يا ذياب
أخشى أن يكون قد أصابَهُ عارضٌ ما .

"Kahraman is late today, Diab.
I am afraid something wrong happened,"
said Dana.

ثم يقفزُ الطفلانِ فرحاً :

لقد وصل كهرمان.

ـ لقد قلقنا عليك كثيراً.

يجيب كهرمان :

ـ أنا آسف..

لم أستيقظ لأنني متعب جداً.

Then the two kids jumped joyfully!
Kahraman is here.
"We were worried about you," they said.
"I am sorry, I was so tired.
I couldn't wake up," said Kahraman.

دانت وذياب مهتمان بصحت صديقهما
- هل رأيت يا دانت كم هو متعَبٌ كهرمان؟
- نعم، نريد أن نساعده ..
- ولكن كيف ؟؟

Dana and Diab seemed concerned
about their friend's health
Kahraman is so tired Dana," said Diab.
"Yes, he is.
We want to help him," said Dana.
"But how?"

ذياب ودانة يفكران :
الكهرباء والإنارة أصبحا مُهمين.
المصباح، والألعاب الإلكترونية، والكمبيوتر
كلها تعمل بالكهرباء.
ولا نستطيع الاستغناء عنها.

Dana and Diab are thinking.
Electricity and lights are important
Electricity is used for lamps, electronic games
and to operate computers.
We can't do without it...

دانة تقفز فرحة :
- لقد وجدتُ حلاً لمساعدة كهرمان.
ذياب أيضاً يقفز فرحاً :
- وأنا أيضاً جاءتني فكرة..

Dana jumps in excitement.
"I found a way to help Kahraman,"
she said.
"Me too," said Diab jumping joyfully too.

- انظر يا ذياب إلى مصباح الطاولة ،
إنه مضاءٌ ونحن لا نستعمله .
ويضيف ذياب :
- وكذلك الكمبيوتر .
يضحكان فرحين : لقد اتفقنا .

"Look Diab to this table lamp. It is turned on,
and we don't use it," said Dana.
"And the computer as well,"
added Diab.
"Agreed!" said the kids, laughing happily.

- أنا سأطفئ المصباح.
- وأنا سأغلق الكمبيوتر ، و "البلي ستيشن" .
يهتف كهرمان سعيداً :
- شكراً دانة ، شكراً ذياب.
تعالا ، إني أدعوكما معي إلى الحديقة ...

"I'll turn off the lamp" said Dana.
"And I'll turn off the computer
and the play-station," said Diab.
"Thanks Dana, thanks Diab,"
said Kahraman cheerfully.
"Come with me to the garden," he said

ذياب ودانة يركضان ويصرخان :
- ماما ، بابا ..
- نعم ، نعم ، ماذا هناك يا أحبتنا؟
- نريد أن نساعد صديقنا كهرمان.
- جيد ونحن نهنئكما! ولكن كيف ؟

"Mum... dad," called Diab and Dana.
- What is up, Dear little ones?
- We want to help our friend, Kahraman.
- Good for you! But how?

– هل تسمحانِ لنا

أن نطفئ الأضواء التي لا نستعملها في المنزل؟

وأن نطفئ التلفاز عندما لا نشاهده؟

ونفتح الستائر لإنارة الصالة؟

Will you allow us

to turn off lights that we don't use at home?

Will you allow us

to turn off the TV when we are not watching it?

and

open curtains to provide light in the hall?

تقول الأم :

- بالطبع يا أولاد ..

ولكن بشرط واحد !!

تتوجس دانة وذياب خوفاً ، ويقولان بصوت خافت :

- وما هو هذا الشرط يا أمَّنا الحبيبة؟

"Sure kids!

You can do this but on one condition only,"

said the mother.

Dana and Diab felt a little worried

"What is it, dear mum?" they said in a low voice.

– شرطنا أن تسمحوا لنا بمساعدتكم في ذلك!

ثم تضحك مازحة ..

وعندها تضحك دانة وذياب بدورهما.

"To allow us to help you,"
she said laughing.
The kids laughed too.

كهرمان يريد أن يلتقي أصدقاءه ذياب ودانة.

تسأله دانة :

– تبدو حزيناً يا كهرمان!

– نعم، ما زال الشغل كثيراً وثقيلاً عليَّ خارج منزلكما .

– نَعِدُكَ يا كهرمان بالاّ نستسلم!

– وسنُساعدك أكثر وأكثر!!

Kahraman wants to meet his friends Diab and Dana.

"You look sad, Kahraman," said Dana.

–Yes, I still have a lot of work outside your house.

– We promise you not to give up Kahraman.

And we will help you more and more!

يضع ذياب ودانة خُطةً لمساعدةِ كهرمان :
- ما رأيكِ يا دانة أن نُشرِكَ أصحابَنا .
- موافقة .. أنا سأهتمُّ بأمرِ صديقاتي ،
وأنتَ يا ذياب أخبِر أصدقائك .

Diab and Dana developed a plan
to help Kahraman.
"How about involving our friends, Dana?" asked Diab.
"Good idea.
I'll tell my friends and you tell yours," said Dana.

يُشغِلُ ذياب الكمبيوتر ،
ويرسل رسائلَ إلكترونيةً لأصحابِه.
أما دانة البارعة في الرسم
فترسمُ لوحةً لتعرِضَها في المدرسة.
الأبُ والأمُ يكلّمانِ أصحابَهما بالهاتف.
الجميع متحمسون...

Diab turned on the computer
and sent emails to his friends.
Dana, the talented painter,
drew a painting to show it in the school.
Mum and dad called their friends.
Every one is excited!

وينمو هناك تعاطفٌ كبير مع كهرمان.
الخطة نجحت..
الجميع بدأ تخفيفَ العمل على كهرمان.
المدرسة أيضاً أخبرتْ جميع الطلاب.

Kahraman gains a great compassion.
The plan works!
Every one starts to work
to ease the heavy burden of Kahraman.
The school informed all the students.

والطلابُ أخبروا أصدقاءَهُم،

والأصدقاءُ كلَّموا أصدقاءهم، وآباءهم...

الكلُّ فَرِحٌ بالمساعدة والمشاركة.

The students told their friends.
The friends told their friends and their parents.
Everyone feels happy
to help and participate.

يأتي كهرمان مسرعاً إلى ذياب ودانة

تسأله دانة :

ـ لماذا تبكي يا كهرمان؟ هل حدث مكروه؟

ـ كلا يا دانة، إنني أبكي من الفرح!

Kahraman hurries to Diab and Dana.
"Why do you cry Kahraman?
What is wrong?" asked Dana.
"Nothing is wrong, Dana.
These are tears of happiness," replied Kahraman.

لم اكن ادري كم تُحِباني أنتِ وذياب،
والآن بمساعدتكم أصبح لي أصدقاء كثيرون!
تتأثر دانة من إحساس كهرمان،
وتنزل دمعتان على خديها...

"I didn't know that you and Diab
love me that much
and now with your help
I have a lot of friends, "he said.
Dana was touched by Kahraman's attitude
Tears swelled up in her eyes.

يقاطع ذياب دانة وكهرمان وينادي :
ـ كفى!! كفكفوا الدموع، ولنفرح!!
سوف نقيم حفلتً كبيرةً لكهرمان
وندعو جميع الأصدقاء!!

"Stop! stop!
No more tears. Let's joy,"
shouted Diab, interrupting Dana and Kahraman.
"We will throw a big party for Kahraman
and invite all friends," he said.

وأخيراً حان موعد الحفل الكبير ،
يقيمونه في حديقة منزل ذياب ودانة .
يتأسف كهرمان لوصوله متأخراً :
ــ عفواً ، ولكنني كنت أتزين للحفلة .

Finally it is the day of the big party
which is held in the garden of Diab and Dana's house.
Kahraman apologizes for arriving late
"Sorry for being late.
I was dressing up for the party," he said.

- كم أنت أنيق!
إنك نجم الحفلة يا كهرمان،
ويجيب كهرمان خجل :
- شكراً يا دانة.

"Look at you!
You are the star of the party, Kahraman".
"Thanks Dana,"
said Kahraman, feeling shy.

الأصدقاء جميعاً يلتفون حول كهرمان
ويقدمون له أجمل الهدايا ...
وهو يضحك من الفرح.

All friends gathered around Kahraman.
They offered him the most beautiful gifts
and he laughs happily.

وفي الصباح التالي،
يستيقظ ذياب ودانة باكراً
وبدل أن يُضيئوا مصابيح الغرفة كعادتهم
تركوا صديقهم كهرمان نائماً.

Diab and Dana woke up early
the next morning.
Instead of turning on the lights in the room
as they used to do,
they left their friend Kahraman asleep.

وفتحوا ستارة النافذة
فأضاءت الشمس غرفتهما ،
آه ،
ما أجمل ضوء النهار!!

They opened the curtains, and
the sunlight spreads over the room.
Oh!
How beautiful daylight is!

وفيما ينام كهرمان
محتضناً كل الهدايا ؛
تمنى ذياب ودانة لصديقهما كهرمان
أجمل الأحلام...

النهاية

And while Kahraman sleeps,
hugging all his gifts,
Diab and Dana wish their friend Kahraman
the sweetest dreams...

The End

Your Comments

Would you like to express
your love for kahraman
in writing?

تعليقاتكم

هل ترغبون في التعبير
عن حبكم لكهرمان
في الكتابة؟
شكرا يا أصدقائي!
أحبكم...

To help Kahraman,
write what would you like
to do with Diab and Dana?

Thank You,
My Friends!
I Love You ...

لمساعدة كهرمان،
أكتبوا ما تحبون فعله
مع ذياب ودانة؟

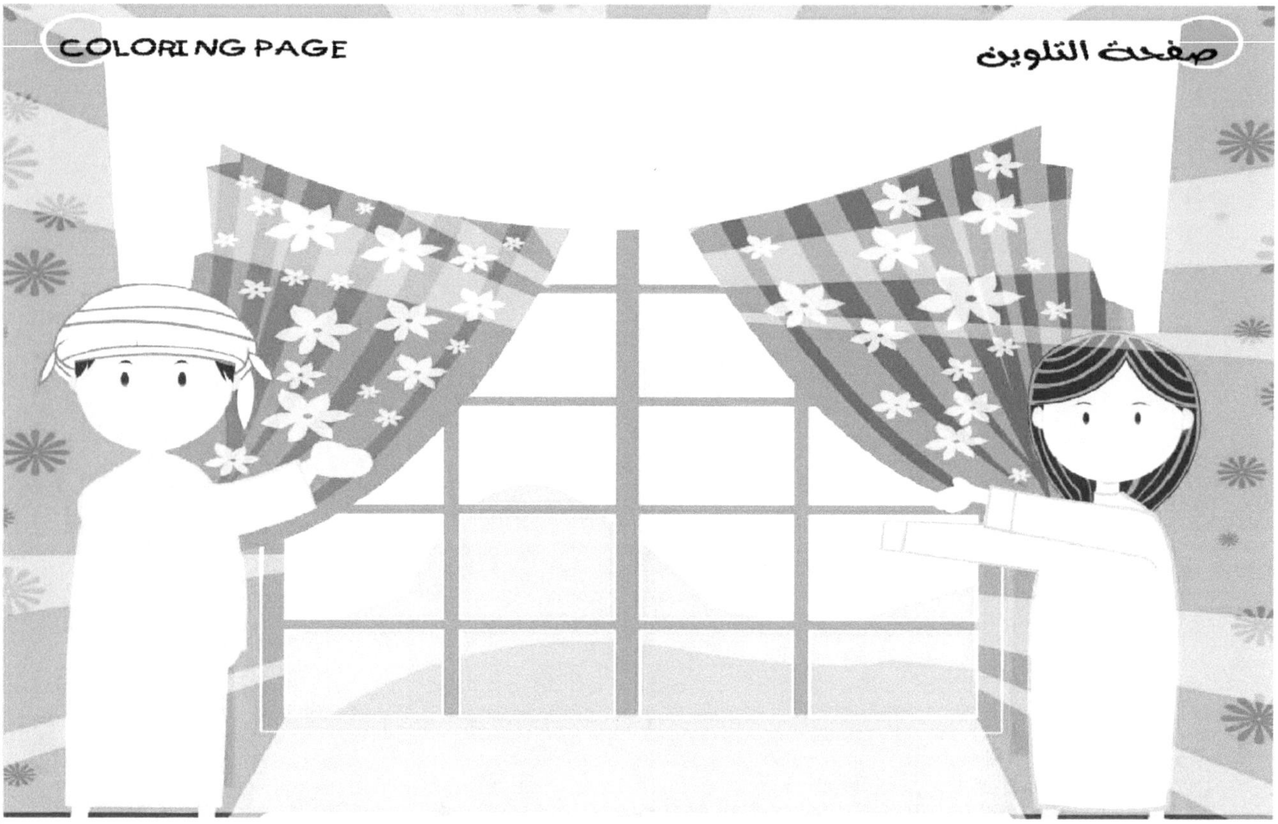

COLORING PAGE

صفحة التلوين

COLORING PAGE

صفحة التلوين

COLORING PAGE
صفحة التلوين
COLORING PAGE
صفحة التلوين

COLORING PAGE صفحة التلوين

COLORING PAGE صفحة التلوين

GIFTS NURTURE LOVE
تهادوا تحابوا
زياب ودانة مع كهرمان
DIAB AND DANA WITH KAHRAMAN
FRIENDS OF NATURE SERIES
سلسلة أصدقاء الطبيعة
Dr. Bassam Klink
Warda Sulaiman

DRAWING PAGE

صفحة الرسم

DRAWING PAGE

صفحة الرسم

DRAWING PAGE

صفحة الرسم

DRAWING PAGE

صفحة الرسم

DRAWING PAGE

DRAWING PAGE

صفحة الرسم

DRAWING PAGE

صفحة الرسم

DRAWING PAGE

صفحة الرسم

DRAWING PAGE

صفحة الرسم

DRAWING PAGE

DRAWING PAGE

صفحة الرسم

DRAWING PAGE   صفحة الرسم

DRAWING PAGE

صفحة الرسم